# RETIRE ON RENT

*All the Benefits of Real Estate
Without the Pain*

*by Michael Drew*

Copyright © 2015 Michael Drew

Published by MG Publishing

220 N 1300 W Ste 4, Pleasant Grove, UT 84062

Michael Drew

6215 N College Ave Indianapolis, IN 46220
(317) 900-4228

Printed in the United States of America

*Dedication:*

*To Dad.*

*Life is too short,*
*thanks for pointing me*
*in the right direction.*

*I so miss you.*

# CONTENTS

# LIFE IS SHORT

Have you noticed how some days just seem to stick out from the others?

Honestly, couldn't tell you what I did the day before or the day after that afternoon when I had lunch with my Dad.

Dad had just taken off work and was getting ready to go in for treatment. The melanoma cancer had spread to his brain and lungs. It really didn't look good.

I can see that something was weighing heavy on his mind. I didn't blame him. Who wouldn't have a lot on their mind. His shoulders slumped forward. My own heart broke. I thought to myself, "I'm too young to be without my Dad!"

"How can I ease the burden of a man who has taken care of me and our family so selflessly?" I asked myself.

Dad had married his high school sweetheart, Mom. He never made a ton of money, but he'd plodded along, honest as the day is long, doing the very best he could to provide and plan for the future.

Dying of cancer in his early 60's wasn't ever in the plan. I knew this brave man wasn't thinking about his own death, but about his bride.

---

## "Dad, I'll take care of Mom."

---

His gaze raised from the food in front of him. Immediately I saw his shoulders relax. His furrowed brow softened and relief poured over his face.

"Thanks, Michael. Thank you. I know you will."

I was 31, with two young children and full of unfulfilled promises. To be perfectly frank I was scared.

Mom, like any baby boomer, would want her independence. We weren't going to stick her in the basement. Her baby boomer pride wouldn't want to live with us either. Yet she and Dad didn't have enough saved up for her to live off for very long.

I had some experience in the stock market, but I wasn't going to risk my Mother's future. I had to figure out what I could do to make sure my own Mother could retire with dignity, not relying on her children. I had to figure out how to create real Mailbox Money without going for risky investments.

What I learned on my journey to keep the promise I made to my own Father as he faced his own mortality is what you hold in your hands now.

I've used my approach to help other widows, retirees, brand new parents and baby boomers alike, as well as successful people from all walks of life to "Retire On Rent".

I look forward to pointing you in the right direction as you read this book.

If I left it there, I'd feel like I let you down. If you have questions that come up as you read and think about how you'll Retire On Rent, give my office a call. Tell my assistant that you're reading my book and have questions you'd like to discuss with me regarding a possible 'Blueprint'.

If you use those secret words, they will schedule a time for us to chat. There is nothing I love more than helping folks realize the reality that I was blessed to be able to create for my own Mother.

I wish you the best and hope you too find peace in this book knowing you too can Retire On Rent!

# Chapter 1

# THE DREAM

You've probably heard that real estate is one of the most widely held investment classes of millionaires.

In 2014, Bloomberg News reported that over 77% of United States millionaires held real estate and of those surveyed, real estate was the most favored investment for its short term and long term benefits.

The Oracle of Omaha, Warren Buffett, wishes he could have more residential real estate, but didn't know how to scale it.

The idea that real estate, and specifically residential real estate, is the key to unlocking the kind of returns investors want, isn't new.

You can go back centuries to find examples if you like, but it really isn't necessary.

Today, savvy individuals are discovering what I had to learn the hard way...that rental income can be completely passive and massively profitable.

## *You just have to do it right.*

Do it wrong, and you'll be moaning the misery of tenants and toilets.

Do it right, and you'll be enjoying truly passive income with rates of return that will make anyone jealous. If anything, it may be a challenge to NOT talk about how great your investments are doing.

## *That's a good problem to have.*

Of course right now, the idea of telling others about your exciting new investment of residential rental properties might not sound all that feasible. After all, the idea of retiring on rental income is nothing new and quite frankly, it isn't too sexy...on the surface!

While I haven't sold any tech companies I created, and I haven't won the lottery, I have been fortunate to make quite a bit of "earned income". And believe me, it was all earned. I had to work my butt off.

When I was younger I was, admittedly, a bit arrogant and cocky. The world was mine and I was going to conquer it by 35. But my cockiness cost me quite a bit and my arrogance ended up humbling me.

## *The biggest humbling experience of my life...*

The biggest humbling experience of my life was when I promised my dying Father I'd take care of my Mother.

There was no more time to talk a big game. There was no more time to just dream big. I had to put up. I had to take care of business. It's times like those that cause you to dig deep and look around with a new sense of purpose.

I'd been trying to get rich for a few years at that point. To be perfectly honest, I was doing all right but when it came to helping Mom, I was lost.

I went for the goal of passive income because of the many failures I experienced in seeking a high annual earned income and how little of that money I was actually keeping.

I went from company to company. I was involved in the stock market and had a career in public speaking. I made a very nice income from both of those industries. I had some good years and some bad years, but that all lead me to where I am today. In my 40's and on track to completely Retire On Rent in a few years.

And when I say retire, I don't mean work at Starbucks. I mean retire with the lifestyle I want, all expenses paid for by rent.

Let's be honest, saving money takes daily discipline, and I'll give you that it's important, but an actual plan to earn $5,000, $10,000, $20,000 per month or more FROM your assets is different.

From a young age, I was fascinated with making money, yet until I found real estate, I didn't know how exciting a seemingly simple investment could be.

**Think about it - as you get older and older, your exposure to risk should go where? Up or Down?**

I also didn't know how many pitfalls come along with rental real estate for those that don't know what they are getting into.

---

*"Make my money work for me."*

---

Today, I have quite a few clients. Folks who have realized the dream of truly passive income, in large part due to rental income.

When I first chat with a potential client, inevitably the same conversation comes up time and time again when they say: "Michael, what I really want, is for the money I've saved to work as hard as I did when I earned it in the first place. Then, I want it to continue to work for me."

All too often I see people who think they're "retired" but who are actually tied to managing their investments. It could be stocks, apartments, or a business that they own. What they are saddled up with is a part-time job, but what they really wanted was...

## Mailbox Money

Mailbox Money is a term that was made popular by some of the real estate investment gurus from the 1980s.

Mailbox Money is passive monthly income from your assets that is mailed to you each month. Mailbox Money is, to some people, like a unicorn.

They tried using all the techniques that gurus were teaching, but never could achieve true passive income from their assets. There always seemed to be a lot of work to get there and even more work to maintain it. For many who sought to create Mailbox Money from their investments, it seemed to be an unachievable goal.

But I have good news! Mailbox Money is achievable and I and the folks I work with are living proof!

True passive income, whether you're on vacation in another country for three months or at home with your family is possible, and  rentals, I believe, are the way to achieve it.

How much is enough?

We all like the idea of passive income. However, how much we need our retirement plan to create, depends on our lifestyle and wants.

True retirement from passive income is achieved when the income from your assets exceeds your monthly "lifestyle expenses" (*not to be confused with living expenses... we all can "get by" with less, but to live the lifestyle we want in retirement is different).*

It's not income from the jobs you work.

It's strictly your passive income from your passive assets.

That is what I mean when I say Retire On Rent.

As I mentioned, a long time ago I fell in love with this idea of retirement from passive income instead of hoping for the government or a corporate pension to be there for me.

I read two GREAT books to get my mindset right: <u>Secrets of the Millionaire Mind</u> by T. Harv Eker and <u>Rich Dad, Poor Dad</u> by Robert Kiyosaki.

I first started to chase this dream of passive income in network marketing. I had mixed success there and then I realized that instead of relying on people generating passive income for my retirement, I would be much better off to rely on assets themselves.

Assets that don't change careers. Assets that don't lose all their value.

Even though I enjoyed helping people in network marketing, when my Dad passed away, I woke up to see a new reality and recognized that I needed to have a solid game plan.

## *When my Dad passed away, I was 31 years old.*

I'm the only son in the family and in our culture there is an unwritten rule that the oldest son takes care of the family if anything happens to Dad.

Shortly before my Dad passed away, when he had stage 4 melanoma (which had spread to his brain and lungs), we had a conversation I will never forget at Applebee's in Crystal Lake, Illinois.

Sitting there in the restaurant with him, he told me he wasn't afraid to die. He felt like he could handle death.

"I've worked hard. I've tried to do right by others. It's just..."

But, there was obviously something that was eating at him. It was something he couldn't bear to say. He didn't have enough money saved up to take care of Mom for the rest of her life.

As a man, he felt he had let his wife down and it was harder for him than facing death. That's the kind of man my Dad was. I could tell he didn't want to place the burden on me, but he didn't know what else to do.

When I told him with stern confidence, my shoulders back and determination in my voice, "I will take care of Mom!", relief overtook him. He could leave this life in peace. He knew that I would make sure Mom had all she needed. He knew that he could pass that responsibility on to me.

## 31 and Clueless...

Leaving that conversation, I faced the haunting reality that at 31 years old, nothing in my experience, nothing I had access to, could ever take care of Mom to the point that she wouldn't have to worry about money for the rest of her life.

You can imagine, this reality took me from being the arrogant young man I was, to realizing I would have to step up and take things more seriously if I was going to keep my promise to my dying Dad.

The first thing I did was make sure she would retain ownership of her home when Dad passed away. I wanted her to retain integrity and autonomy of her money.

Now I wasn't a total moron. I'd done pretty well, so I looked at what I did know and then I looked to apply it to an area that would be safe enough to take care of Mom.

## The Right System and The Right People

The stock market was just too risky for Mom's situation, so I started to look for a system out there that I could plug into where the assets my Dad left behind would generate enough income to provide for Mom each month.

Honestly, there wasn't enough money left behind to take care of Mom through retirement if all I had to hope for a 3%-5% annual return on the money.

I needed a system that would work an asset class that had relative stability to it. That was the easy part. Real estate, even with the wild ride we saw in 2006-2012, is still on track to average 3.5% appreciation year over year, over the last 40 years.

You can't get more stable than that. But Mom couldn't eat real estate. She couldn't wear it. She couldn't drive it around. So how do I make it pay her?

**Rent**.

---

*But everyone knows that rentals are a royal pain.*

---

You have to get the *right* people in the house. If something goes wrong, you have to pay for it. It sounds more like a job, than passive income.

Could rental income really be what Mom needed?

### Ray's Real Business

As a side note, if you asked Ray Kroc what business he was in, you would have been surprised by his answer.

To be fair, at first he thought he was in the selling of a business system, the franchise business.

But when he met the financial genius, Harry Sonnenborne, Ray became convinced that he was not in the hamburger or business system business at all, but rather, he was in the real estate business.

McDonalds would purchase or lease the land each franchise would be located on and then lease the land to the franchisee, or take the franchise fees, whichever was greater.

The secret to his success has clues to your own retirement success...

# Making Rental Passive

If you desire true "Mailbox Money" without all the pain and work of investing in real estate, a proven system is the answer.

It's kind of like McDonalds, this whole system that is based out of Oak Brook, Illinois. Back in 1961, Ray Kroc purchased McDonalds and it's systems from the McDonald brothers for 2.7 million dollars. Today McDonalds is worth 95 Billion dollars.

That system has generated a very nice return on Mr Kroc's investment.

For someone to retire on passive income, they might need or want five or ten thousand dollars a month. Others may want one hundred thousand dollars a month.

That doesn't really matter, it's up to the individual to decide what they want or need in monthly passive income, but what matters is that there are systems behind each of those outcomes that don't include actively doing anything.

To truly Retire On Rent the team and the system is arguably more important than the property itself.

I realize that may sound like a very bold claim, but once you understand the system and what the team that runs it needs to look like, you'll understand completely what I mean.

## A Promise Fulfilled

One of the concerns I had when I was put in charge of managing Mom's assets was that someday she would lose her independence and feel humiliated by having to ask me for money. I didn't want her to be in that position.

Mom had always taken care of me. To this day Mom still buys me Christmas gifts and she still buys my children Christmas gifts. What I wanted was for her to retain the same standard and freedom of living she did when Dad was alive.

Fast forward to today and the system I was able to put in place has cared for her. She enjoys her rental income, and it is going swimmingly well.

Also, it's nice to know that she owns her own assets. She is not dependent on me, she retains her dignity and independence. So my promise to my Dad is being and will continue to be delivered. It doesn't matter if I get hit by a bus, Mom will be taken care of and that makes me feel proud.

The rest of this book is focused on two essential elements of Retire On Rent.

1. The Right System: This includes all the "what's" of Retire On Rent.

2. The Right Team: This includes the people who will do the work to make Retire On Rent a passive activity.

The next three chapters will tell you about *three clients of mine that have utilized the right system and the right team to enhance their retirement plan.

Chapter 2 is about Linda, a 59 year old woman living in Southern California.

Chapter 3 is about Bill, a 47 year old hedge fund manager from Philadelphia.

Chapter 4 is about Heather, a 35 year old successful professional from Northern California.

Chapter 5 is about Dave, a 50 year old with a 401K that he rolled over into rentals.

Chapter 6 on will help you to know how to use the Retire On Rent system.

*Names have been changed to protect the innocent ☺

*Chapter 2*

# TESTING THE WATERS

Linda was 59 years old when we first met.

She had been heavily invested in the stock market and was getting nervous. As she talked with her friends about the market and where it was going, she observed that most folks seem to be investing in the market on "hopium".

Hopium is investing and hoping the investment will go up in value! That wasn't for Linda. She wanted to make a shift that would meet her goals.

You see, Linda didn't want to just squeak by in retirement, and if she were to rely on the stock market alone, she would never reach her goals.

Using a rule of thumb that most financial planners teach, Linda did the math. She knew that in order to not outlive her money, she wouldn't be able to pull more than 4% of her capital each year.

Based on the capital she had available, her current plan wasn't going to work...even with a healthy dose of 'hopium'.

Factor in inflation and a string of bad years in the stock market and anyone on this drug might have second thoughts!

Linda decided to test the waters with two rentals.

She appreciated the ability to own something rather than hope that she wouldn't outlive her money.

Slowly but surely, Linda added to her portfolio between three and four homes each year.

Linda is now going on her fourth year using the Retire On Rent system and she just added her 11th property to her portfolio.

Like most of the folks who are in this stage of life, Linda wanted to move her cash from risker investments and diversify her investments into different asset classes.

Stocks, bonds, annuities, mutual funds are all basically in the same asset class, whereas real estate, equipment leases, and note investing are investments that would limit stock market exposure and also generate passive income.

Those happened to be Linda's primary goals, to limit or spread risk and to start generating predictable, growing, Mailbox Money.

Even during a four year period when real estate has taken a lot of hard knocks, Linda has still been able to hit her retirement goals.

I view rental homes almost as tiny businesses - each of them kicking off monthly income.

Similar to a franchise owner, but without the headaches. Imagine owning 10 or 20 Subways or Pizza places but with no employees, no product, no hours, no overhead, just the monthly income. Yeah, it's that nice.

*Chapter 3*

# MORE LEGS
# TO HIS TABLE

---

While I was more involved in the stock trading industry, I met a gentleman in Philadelphia. To this day, Bill is still very involved in stock market investing; but a few years ago we had a very serious conversation.

Since Bill was actively working in the stock market, it wasn't surprising to discover as we chatted about his portfolio that over 80% of his net worth was literally tied to correlated assets, or correlated classes.

Essentially 80% of his wealth has something to do with the stock market, whether it's a bond, a stock, a mutual fund or an Exchange Traded Fund, they're all correlated to the market, and that made him feel very worried.

At 46 years old, Bill saw that he was getting older, and he saw the need to have other tools in his financial arsenal that are not correlated to the stock market.

If you think about it, it's easy to understand what made Bill so nervous. It is common sense that you don't want to keep all your eggs in one basket.

Bill wanted to diversify into a non-correlated asset fund but not at the expense of making a good rate of return.

The asset class with the least risk, he decided, would be rental real-estate. So he started with one property.

It went so well, that he's added a property every year since he's been working with my team, the Real Estate Done 4 U family, using the Retire On Rent system. He just closed on his third property, with a goal to acquire seven more.

Bill is the type of investor who has very low expenses. What he likes to do with his Mailbox Money is use it to pay off his real estate assets faster.

Even with a 15 year mortgage, using the Retire On Rent system, he still has a positive cash flow on each property!

Because he doesn't need the income currently, each dollar of cash flow is used to pay down the mortgages.

Frequently, when my client doesn't need the cash currently that a rental produces, and wants to add properties quickly to their portfolio they will purchase the rentals with financing.

Because these rentals follow the Retire On Rent approach, they produce cash flow even with a 15 year mortgage. By taking the cash flow and applying to the principle of the mortgages, Bill is able to grow the number of properties he has quicker, allowing for massive leverage.

Have you heard the old adage on how to become a millionaire?

Basically get a million dollars of real-estate debt, and have someone else pay it off.

There is some wisdom to that however, some people do not have the appetite or risk tolerance for that type of debt load and a less aggressive strategy is suited for them.

*Chapter 4*

# YOUNG AND PATIENT

Heather was referred to me by another client.

She had heard about the Retire On Rent system and loved the idea of owning real estate that would produce cash flow.

As a 35 year old chief financial officer of a 30,000 employee company, she decided that even though working in corporate America as a high level executive, there was no way for her to really increase her passive income.

Heather had savings from her high paying corporate job and she could easily qualify for a mortgage, so she started off using the Retire On Rent system to buy a property.

The thrill of receiving checks each month excited her so much, she added a second and third property shortly thereafter.

*I felt like a drug dealer...*

Heather was addicted.

Like so many of my clients, once she got a taste for that Mailbox Money, she couldn't wait to get another property.

I suppose I would feel bad if it wasn't so good.

See, while the stock market is going up and down, a good property that was purchased and managed with the right system keeps generating those monthly rent deposits into your checking account.

Heather once told me, "Well, my stock market investments are going up and down, and with my rentals, I just see consistent direct deposit of rental income. I think I want a couple more of these things."

That's a very common response from clients who use our system.

While our younger clients may enjoy their job, they realize they're not going to get rich in a job; they're going to get rich on what they build with their passive investments.

If you happen to be fortunate enough to be thinking about Retiring On Rent in your 20's or 30's, you have such an advantage as you don't need to take aggressive risks and will see so much greater results from the extra time you have to prepare for retirement.

As much as my more mature clients benefit from the Retire On Rent system, my young clients are also perfect candidates for a plan and a system that's going to work hard to pay off mortgages, while they focus on earning money instead of managing properties.

Our typical client in their 30's has so many other things to pay attention to, because after they're dealing with their hundreds of emails a day and trying to be at the soccer games for the kids, they don't have the bandwidth or energy to go out and fix toilets or anything else that breaks in their rental property.

Therefore, the only thing that makes sense is to have systems in place to avoid all of the negative side of owning real estate. That's why a client like Heather fits perfectly into the Retire On Rent system.

# Chapter 5

# 401K TO IRA

Dave worked for a company for a couple decades and left with a sizable 401k. Being a savvy investor, Dave rolled his 401k into a self-directed IRA.

There are several companies out there now that help people roll their money into self-directed retirement accounts, so Dave's story is becoming more common.

One of the largest companies that assist with these asset rollovers is in Ohio. The last time I heard, they have over 7 billion dollars under management and over 100,000 clients.

In this self-directed IRA, they allow you to invest in and control real estate. This isn't new and has been around for over twenty years.

Dave decided that he wanted a consistent rate of return on his retirement money, and he thought the idea of generating Mailbox Money was great, but he was still relatively young, at 50 years old.

He didn't necessarily need the Mailbox Money right now.

He started his own consulting company and was really enjoying his work. What he wanted to do was have his pot of money earn a consistent monthly income.

So after he rolled that 401K over to a self-directed IRA, we made arrangements to assist Dave in purchasing real-estate inside of his self-directed IRA.

Because Dave is still young, he doesn't pull the money out.

Dave is just building that monthly income up to the time when he decides to retire and knows that there will be several thousand a month coming in. He doesn't need to be worried about pulling that money out faster than it is growing and he doesn't need to risk that money in the stock market.

If you want to put the whole strategy on steroids, use a Roth IRA to own rental real estate. The Roth IRA allows the rents to come in on a tax free basis, improving your cash flow even more.

---

## True Diversification

---

Diversification is not a new theme in any financial planning conversation. If you talk about your retirement plans with your spouse or your child or your parent or your planner, diversification is always a part of that conversation.

However, many planners and "experts" work like what you see in the insurance industry. For example, your insurance agent works for a company like State Farm or Farmers and they only sell you home and auto insurance from their own company, they won't sell you a competitor's insurance.

Likewise, some financial planners only sell you products that generate a commission for them and that are created by their parent company.

Other, potentially more savvy, planners will say, "*Let's put a certain amount of money in the market, but let's go in and develop other streams of income that are non-correlated to the stock market and that way each of these streams of income, or each of these assets, if you will, generate Mailbox Money.*"

Then you might get into some more creative conversations, from self-storage, real estate investment trusts, cellphone towers, etc. that will be generating a monthly income.

Instead of having a hundred thousand dollars or a million dollars just in the stock market or derivatives of the stock market, you have several different asset classes that are each kicking off Mailbox Money individually, either on a monthly or quarterly basis.

Therefore, you can truly structure and reverse-engineer some sort of semblance of a specific monthly income and retirement plan.

Circling back to Dave's plan, when you put that Mailbox Money asset in a retirement account, then the rent just pays directly into the retirement account and it will continue to accumulate each month until you are ready to start drawing from it.

# Chapter 6

# THE RENTAL MYTHS

Before we get into the system, or even where to start, I want to address a few common myths I hear when I talk with someone who is thinking about or has had limited experience with rentals.

These myths can cause undue delay that robs you of passive income that could and should have been yours...of assets that could be working for you now.

## *Myth 1: I need to live close to the rental...just in case.*

This myth is particularly harmful if you live in a market where property values are higher than $100K. Retire On Rent is based in part on basic math. To make the math work in your favor, of course, you need create a combination of income and expenses that will produce cash flow even if you finance the property.

This isn't possible everywhere. If you feel as though you need to live close to the property and you live in say

Irvine, California or New York it's going to be nearly impossible to make the math work in your favor.

When I press new clients on why they feel that the property needs to be close, it comes out that there is a sense of responsibility for the care of the property.

This is very noble, but completely unnecessary and the source of rentals becoming a liability verses a vehicle to truly passive income.

I'll give you permission right now, just in case you find yourself feeling like you have to keep your fingers on the property, to let go. Confidence to let go will come as you have confidence in the team that acquires, rehabilitates, rents out and maintains your properties.

A wise friend and mentor of mine, Kris, says: "If you want a job done right then DON'T do it yourself". Remember, let's begin with the end in mind here. Do your own due diligence. As any good leader knows, in order to grow and scale, you must develop leaders. This part of your life is supposed to give you time freedom longer-term. Your weekends are for your family.

---

## *Myth 2: I need a lot of money to get started.*

---

I won't lie. If you have a bunch of money to work with everything is easier. But the idea that you need a bunch of money to get started, normally is connected to the first myth.

If you believe you need to purchase rentals near you, then by extension you probably need quite a bit more to buy or finance the properties. Additionally, the cash flow will create a lower cap rate making it a less lucrative venture.

When you combine these two factors, it's easy to understand why folks will put off Retiring On Rent because they believe it will take more capital to start the process and they lack a system.

As you'll learn in more depth later, the ideal price range for properties is $50-100K. This price range makes the cash flow you want possible.

---

*Myth 3: $50-100K properties are slums.*

---

My friend Ryan was born and raised in San Diego. His father was a general contractor building custom homes across the Western United States.

He said when he heard of homes that sold for $50-100K, he was bewildered at how that was even possible. "It seems like the cost of the materials should be more than $100K for a single family home that size."

The reality is the price of a home that will rent well depends on the area where the home is located. Our approach to Retire On Rent dictates that you must select properties in areas where the values are expected to be supported 30 years in the future.

This means we have to look for neighborhoods that are going to be desirable now and in the future. Places folks in the area will want to live.

Additionally, the neighborhoods must be predominately owner occupied over the long haul.

The end result is you end up with solid properties in good neighborhoods that will keep their value and stay occupied.

# Chapter 7

# WHAT SHOULD I DO?

A savvy financial planner friend once shared this analogy with me about what it really means to diversify.

He compares your retirement investment strategy to a table. The more "legs" it has, the more stable and secure it will be.

So one leg on the table might be stocks, bonds or mutual funds. Those are all in the same asset class. Another might be an investment commercial or residential real estate.

The point is, the table with one leg is much more likely to be toppled and does not provide as secure of a foundation as a table with multiple legs.

I don't rely on the stock market only, because I want to be safe. Remember my story. My goal was to take care of my Mom with very little risk.

*Is it possible to Retire On Rent
as the only leg to your table?*

Absolutely. I fully believe that it's possible, but that being said, remember diversification?

I just want you to reduce your risk as you get older and develop an appetite for ideas that produce passive income...whatever they may be.

With rental income you take your gross rents, minus maintenance, vacancy, insurance, and taxes and you're going to end up with your net income. You're then going to determine one of two things, *"I can definitely retire on X amount of money coming in on a monthly basis"*, or *"I can't."*

Some people will say, *"You know what, rent is only going to be one of the legs on my financial table. I'm going to have pension income, dividends, etc or I'm relying on X per month of social security income (if it is still around when you retire)."*

---

## Why is **now** the very best time to get started with rental income?

---

There's a video that was very popular about real estate investing in the last couple years in which Warren Buffet said the following:

*"If I could buy a couple thousand single-family homes and manage them, it would be one of the things I would do with my money right now. The difficult part is having the system to manage them."*

Warren Buffet was onto something ;)

It took years of fine tuning to create the Retire On Rent System including how to manage acquisitions, identify how to "proactively rehab", attract good tenants, and make managing the property and tenant a much simpler and successful process.

The real secret to the entire system is a series of tight feedback loops and systems with a common goal in mind... Mailbox Money for the investor.

## Why should I invest in real estate now and why should I use the Retire On Rent system?

In the beginning, with our first hundred properties that we put through the Retire On Rent System, we made mistakes...but we made mistakes with our *own* money.

Now that we've ironed out the wrinkles and made the system a humming machine, we have the great pleasure of providing clients with the benefits of our learning curve... turn-key properties.

When I talk with folks who have been thinking about getting into rentals, or maybe had a good experience in the past, but are worried it was beginner's luck, they normally have a few common misconceptions.

## You start building your wealth the day you get started.

So now is the best time for you, regardless of where you are or what the economy is doing. You've heard the old saying, "*Don't wait to buy real estate, buy real estate and wait.*"

Our approach is not focused on appreciation, that's just a huge bonus. The focus is on cash flow.

By acquiring properties in the right places, managed by the right system, they will produce cash flow from day one and if there is any mortgage, the plan is to have the rent from the property itself pay off the mortgage for you.

The compound effect of this is where the old saying, "Don't wait to buy real estate, buy real estate and wait" comes into play.

There aren't any investments out there that have as much upside, with as much mitigated risk and government incentives as real estate.

---

## Which way is the best way for me to invest in real estate?

---

Of course, to identify what is best for you, we'll want to walk through what is "*acceptable*" and what is "*ideal*." These questions will help you determine the best path for you.

1. If you are looking to Retire On Rent, do you want to have a part-time or full-time job managing real estate during retirement?

2. Do you want to take the gamble and on your own: analyze neighborhoods, determine the best rent to acquisition costs, and acquire the property in "as is" condition?

3. Do you feel confident buying a property after determining if it has hidden issues?

4. Are you competent at rehabbing a home, while keeping the project on budget and on time?

5. Are you excited by the thought of becoming a market expert, a rehab expert, and a tenant screening expert?

6. Do you enjoy things like drywall repairs, fixing toilets, and collecting rent?

7. Do you enjoy spending a few weekends a month managing properties?

If you answered "Yes" to at least three of the above questions, you have the interest and some energy to try out managing a passive rental income opportunity on your own. Good for you!

But, if you answered "No" to three or more of the questions above, you'll be happy to know that our strategy gives you the peace of mind of simply putting your money to work for you to generate Mailbox Money.

One of the keys to determining how using my Mailbox Money, Retire On Rent approach fits into your plan is by reverse engineering your ideal retirement scenario.

If you are new to the term "*reverse engineer*", you can think of it this way...

When my friends compete in marathons, they know that in a future date they will be running 26.2 miles as quickly and efficiently as possible.

They often have a time goal in mind as well. The runner will start with the end in mind and work backward on what it will take to achieve the goal.

Nowadays you can go online and search Google for a marathon training program. You simply enter the date of your event, and based on the amount of time you have before the marathon, the program plots your weekly running mileage plan.

For example, to work up to running 26.2 miles, you'll probably be instructed to run two to three miles a day during the week and then do a long run on the weekend.

This is exactly how you can approach your retirement and your wealth. We start with your end goal in mind and then proactively plot your course.

Do you want to be actively involved in creating the retirement you want or are you going to take a dose of "hopium" and just wait and see what happens?

Engaging in this process on your own requires that you love managing rental real estate.

If your dream is to spend your time in your rental properties and managing the process, then taking your own path vs. using ANY system could be more fulfilling and profitable for you.

If you answered yes to 6 or more of the earlier questions, then doing this on your own is your dream and you probably feel that you hardly need, for example, a property manager to aid in your journey.

For me, I have kids and the sexiest wife on the planet. I have nieces and nephews and I live in a fun and super active community. I enjoy spending time with friends and entertaining. More importantly, I also know my weaknesses.

For example, is it possible for me to change the oil on my vehicle? The answer is probably.

Will I save money verses taking my car to the shop for an oil change? It's likely.

Am I the best qualified person to do that? The answer would be absolutely not.

Could I do something wrong that could cost me a lot more money to fix on my car? For me, it's almost guaranteed.

Would I rather spend that time with my family and friends enjoying this life or relaxing? Absolutely! I know that my time is better invested in other things and more important priorities in my life.

Therefore, I pay the small fee to have someone change my oil. I take ten to twenty minutes and go into the shop. They open up the garage doors and while they are changing my oil, they'll even change my air filter while they are at it, saving me time and another trip.

I do not begrudge the mechanic because I pay a small fee for him to change my oil.

Taking my car to the shop to have my oil changed is like my Retire On Rent system- it is in place to take care of the needs that go along with rental real estate.

This, too, is how I also approach investing and in particular, property management and retirement.

Is managing the process something that many people could do on their own? Sure.

After doing it for three to five years, you will have learned a lot and can begin to probably put your own systems in place; but during that learning curve, you will make mistakes that will cost you time and money.

Plus, you'll be spending your time managing your "passive" income opportunity with repairs, renters, and issues as they arise.

Is going through that learning curve by spending your precious time and losing some of your hard earned money that way really something you want to do?

This is what scares off most people from this asset class, a horror story or two. If you do not have a system in place, a 30 day vacancy can turn into a 90 pretty quickly, which just destroyed 25% of your potential annual rent.

Like changing your oil, opt to have a professional do it for you. We've built a great property management team that works closely with the team that rehabs the property.

Generally, we will use the same quality of materials in each of the properties that we manage.

That way, if the Property Management team gets called for a plumbing issue and we find out it's related to the wax ring on the toilet, the repair team is familiar with the issue and has the parts already in the truck, ready to go.

They grab the parts, fix the problem and before you know it, they're done, all while you're out golfing or spending with with the family.

That's the kind of retirement I want, not one that I have to show up for every little issue that may arise.

---

## Reverse engineer your retirement

---

By now, you're getting pretty clear on whether you are up for being a landlord and handy repair person or if you prefer to have true passive Mailbox Money. The next thing to consider is how much money do you want to retire on and what will that require of you now?

The first step is to determine your desired monthly passive income. Let's start with an example. If someone says "I want to build a $5,000, $10,000 or $20,000 a month passive income", we need to consider where they live. If they live in California, Florida or Boston for example, then they're not going to buy real estate in those areas, because those areas are not going to be the best areas of opportunity for rental income vs. cost of acquisition.

They'll want to buy in the Midwest somewhere.

Now after considering how much monthly income you want to have in retirement, the next step in your Retire On Rent plan, just like in a marathon, depends on how much time you have left to prepare before you want to retire.

Let's assume, like many Americans, you plan on retiring at age 65. I like to break up the starting points into four-quarters. Depending on which quarter of pre-retirement life you find yourself, you'll use a different strategy.

What I mean by that is that most people spend 40 years making money, from age 25 to age 65.

| 1st QTR | 2nd QTR | 3rd QTR | 4th QTR |
| --- | --- | --- | --- |
| 25-35 | 36-45 | 46-55 | 56-65 |

When you divide up each ten years into a quarter; 25 to 35 is the first quarter, 36 to 45 is the second quarter, 46 to 55 is the third quarter and 56 to 65 is the fourth quarter.

If you're really serious about retiring on rent and you're late into your third quarter or already in your fourth quarter, but only have $50K in retirement assets saved up, then you're behind the eight ball.

We're going to have to take a different approach with you than we would with someone who has $50K in retirement who is in their first or second quarter of pre-retirement life.

## Your Personal Plan

Are you wondering what your plan could look like?

Text **PLAN** to **(317) 900-4228** and you'll be guided through the process of discovering the plan to Retire on Rent that's right for you.

# Chapter 8

# A PROVEN SYSTEM

**True passive rental income, AKA "Mailbox Money", is possible when you have the right team, using the right system.**

The overall key principle of Mailbox Money is really the people and the property management.

**The 5 Keys of Retire On Rent**

Property Selection
Property Acquisition
Property Rehabilitation
Property Management
Audit and Accounting

Let me give an example, and I'll go on to use those specific points later, but you must have systems that are run by people, ideally it's a family owned and operated business.

A perfect example of one of the pitfalls of property management is hiring someone who doesn't actually own or manage any of their OWN properties.

They don't know how to limit the cost the same way someone does who has hundreds of homes of their own which they bought, rehabbed and manage.

A property manager who is also an owner, someone who owns the same rental real estate that their clients are investing in, has a vested interest in the success of the system that they are putting your property in.

The second pitfall for most small property management companies is that they don't have their own team of repairmen. They don't have trucks fixing the property one block over, so they don't have the flexibility that a property manager with a full-time team has.

## Property Selection

Picking the right neighborhood for tenants, and for long term value.

A common question I get from investors is, *"How do you figure out what properties are going to be best for high rents, good tenants, and fewer problems?"*

One of the biggest mistakes that people make in the property selection is they buy *"cheap"* homes.

When I'm talking about the system, I'm talking about the team at the same time, because if your team isn't involved in the same markets, then they're not impacted by mistakes made.

When they are, they make sure they don't make mistakes.

It's sort of like buying chicken from the grocery store. Cheap chicken may not taste as good, it's often not as healthy as it will usually have more fat, include the bone and skin, but it's $1.99 a pound.

There is a reason why it's $1.99 a pound, and why lean trimmed organic is so much more expensive. It's because one is better quality than the other.

Sure, they'll both fill you up, but one will be easier to prepare and healthier for you in the long run.

When you buy "cheap" real estate (*under $30,000 - $45,000 in the Midwest*) and have these high in the sky hopes, don't be so shocked when you have to deal with constant turnover of tenants, vandalism, and high repair costs, etc.

The bottom line is, too good to be true "cheap" properties have high risks.

It's kind of like gambling in Vegas. Go ahead and buy cheap properties only with money that you're willing to lose and that's it.

If you lose it, then you'll walk away, just like when you lose money in Vegas as you knew the odds were not in your favor when you went into it.

So that's the first thing to remember:

Don't buy cheap houses.

The sad thing is, that is where a lot of investors choose to get started. Then what happens is you might have good performance for about six months or a year, but then something goes wrong.

Stop and think for a minute about what types of tenants you would attract to live in a $20K-$30K home. For the $450 a month in rent, even though it looks good on paper, that type of house is not going to bring in your highest return, because it won't bring you a stable, consistently paying tenant.

When you have the eventual turn over and vacancy, you're more likely to have major damage to repair, like vandalism, stolen AC units, and stripped copper, to name a few.

My friend Ryan, whom I mentioned earlier, went this route before he learned about the Retire On Rent system.

He and his brother picked up three of these "cheap homes" with hopes of renting them out for a high ROI.

Before they could even get tenants in two of them, the copper was stripped out and the homes were vandalized. The total repair costs to those two houses totaled nearly 50% of the original acquisition cost!

The third property worked out alright but the cash flow across the three properties is half of what it would have been if they had purchased one property with the Retire On Rent system. You can imagine how disappointed they felt.

Remember when you go cheap, what you generally attract is a tenant who will likely not take care of the property and the profits are eaten up in fixing up the property every time you have turn over.

Learn from my mistakes and the mistakes of thousands of other people we've helped. Avoid the "cheap house" lure as it will likely only bring you headaches and lost profit.

Unfortunately, it costs people $50,000-$100,000 or more in some cases, to learn this lesson. When that happens, many people get a bad taste in their mouth and will sign off on investing in real estate altogether.

What we've learned in creating the Retire On Rent system to find the best properties is that you begin by looking at the nearby schools.

If you're going to find a good tenant, they usually have a family or want to live in a good area with families. Those families with children are often most concerned with having their child enrolled in a good school.

Usually, where there are good schools there will also be nearby shopping, nearby hospitals, and a community.

Stay out of the areas where the schools aren't great.

I've thought a lot about the tenant in my acquisition, rehab, screening and management processes.

The quality of the tenant contributes to the success of the entire system, so I want good tenants who pay every month, maintain the home with pride, fix little things themselves, while having a great rent to acquisition cost ratio.

All of this study has led me to only buy single family homes. Does that surprise you?

I don't buy duplexes, quads or apartments. I know there are many out there who promote this approach, but I have learned my lessons the hard way and have different goals. Remember my start, the investment had to be secure for my own Mother. I can't afford to have irregularities in the cash flow.

Good families, the kind that rent single family homes, will stay in a home for years...that's what I want. I admit I'm biased and I have a friends that have gone the multi-unit route, but most of them have been exponentially a higher maintenance endeavor than single family homes.

When's the last time you were in an apartment where you thought, "*I really enjoy sharing a wall with someone else so they can hear everything going on in my life.*"

I can go share a wall at the Marriott, but I don't want to do that every night, that's only out of necessity.

Good tenants prefer privacy, a nice yard, and place to make their home for their family.

From my experience, a single-family home, on a longer-term basis, is going to more consistently produce income with fewer vacancies in between tenants.

Property selection also needs to include consideration of the location's impact on my ability to market the property to potential tenants.

With Real Estate Done 4U, we think about the location of other properties in the system that will give us the upper-hand to keep the properties occupied.

If you're going alone and picking up properties one or two at a time, you're at a disadvantage when it comes to getting the best tenants.

A great team will know what type of clientele is attracted to the neighborhood. They know who they are marketing to and how to attract them so you have great tenants who feel at home in the area.

When we look to acquire a home, we look for neighborhoods that have the look and feel of being predominantly owner occupied. That usually means that 75% or greater of the homes in the area are owner-occupied.

An easy way to know that is to look at the yards. Most renters don't traditionally put much into landscaping the homes they are living in yet homeowners take pride in their homes and maintain the landscape.

Another thing to look for is the quality of the vehicles in the driveways. I know you can't always judge a book by its cover, so the cars in the neighborhood aren't a sure bet but the average middle-class worker will usually drive a nice, well-kept car they can afford.

---

## *What impact does the local job market in a city have on your property selection?*

---

One of the keys for having a large field of possible great rentals to pick from is finding a capital city. That's number one.

I've found that being in an area with government jobs, such as is the case with Indianapolis where my clients and

I have had tremendous success, lends itself to a more stable economy.

Having all the state level government jobs in the capitol has the tendency to flow into the surrounding suburbs.

Another thing to keep in mind is: How business friendly is the city, county, and state? A city has the ability to give tax incentives or tax-breaks, to companies that will relocate there or that provide business there. Some cities will seek to attract certain types of businesses.

Ideally, what you want to look for in a city is employment where there is diversity of employers and industries that would offer more stability should one sector of the local economy be impacted by national or global changes.

For example, you would not want to be involved long term in Detroit, because employment from the automobile related industry has a great influence on the rental industry.

Even the wiring harness companies in Ohio felt the pain when the auto makers hit hard times in early 2005 - and virtually every other auto-related industry.

What you are going to look for are counties with various industries and a diverse economic base,  built around a strong government sector base. To simplify it even more, we are looking for strong counties that don't have much volatility in the job market.

Once you have determined a strong economy and good local job market, there are still other factors that will make an area less desirable for our goal of retiring on rental cash flow.

If you take San Diego County as an example, you have a great local economy, with biotech companies, the top three golf companies, defense contractors (the list of strong industries could go on and on) and a strong government sector, including several military bases.

The problem with San Diego County is that the high home prices compared to the rental rates don't fit so well within the formula required to earn a great ROI. So San Diego County is not an option that meets the proven requirements in the Retire On Rent program.

Investors throughout Southern California are "*banking*", in part, on the house to appreciate. If that does not happen, their negative cash-flow investment quickly turns into a horrible idea.

Even though I personally really enjoy the sunshine in San Diego, there's no way that I could achieve the same net income from investing in single-family homes there.

San Diego would not pencil out and the Retire On Rent model just wouldn't work in those parts of the country without taking the risk of "hoping" for appreciation to make up the significant difference.

In Southern California, most rentals will yield a 5%-7% capitalization rate.

In layman terms, that means that for every $100K you invest in acquiring the home, you can expect $5,000-$7,000 a year in rental income.

Compare that with the 8%-12% that I aim to achieve in my target markets.

What we are looking for is anywhere between a 12-15% gross rent or in other words, each year we would like to receive 12%-15% of the purchase price in rental income.

While there are many people buying rentals in areas that have similar 5%-7% yields like in San Diego County, there is one main difference why you should invest in rentals in the Midwest.

One of the main reasons for investing in rentals located in great counties throughout the Midwest is **CASHFLOW**.

Some of the rentals in other parts of the country are going to be considered stronger, but you're going to assume some added risk.

The numbers won't be the same and as I mentioned earlier, a lot of those rentals are counting on appreciation in order to make a similar return to what we will have over the same 5-10 year period in the Midwest.

## Buying for Appreciation vs Buying for Cash Flow

When you buy rental real-estate in the right market with the right system, you're not banking on appreciation, its just a bonus.

In fact, any good book on real estate rental investing will teach you that you're banking on cash flow, as that is predictable and can be counted on, whereas, as we've seen, you can't always count on appreciation.

If you are in your first or second quarter of life (25-45 years old), you have more flexibility in your choice about risk.

But as you get older and near your fourth quarter of life, your focus should be strictly on the best cash-flow for your money, rather than hope for appreciation to fund your retirement.

What you'll find after you do your research, is that on the coasts (East and West) your real-estate is typically more expensive and also more susceptive to market fluctuations both negative and positive.

Also, on the coasts you'll often see that the numbers won't usually work out for a great rate of return for a cash flowing property.

In some of the coasts, like Florida for example, you'll have very high insurance costs. In other areas, you will have high property taxes. You'll have higher costs to such a degree that you will not be able to own a rental property that generates a good rate of return.

This is what brought me back to the Midwest time and time again in the beginning.

In the interior of the United States you will find that a capital city won't usually have high property taxes and insurance costs.

---

## My Current Favorite City with all the ingredients is Indianpolis

---

My philosophy has always been *"I want to take care of Mom."*

My Mom didn't have a million dollars to invest.

Therefore, I wanted to diversify what she had available to invest, so investing in a home that was over $100,000 to generate 7% a year didn't make sense for her at all.

That definitely disqualified Mom from buying homes in the nice cities on the coasts, because those numbers didn't make sense for her situation.

It doesn't make sense for cash flow for most people's situations.

It didn't make sense for her security, because there's more volatility in those markets.

Even though those markets may have had some of the other positive property selection criteria I look for with the Retire On Rent system, it would have invalidated the actual goals of the system:

*To produce a safer, more reliable rate of return that could be counted on for low maintenance "Mailbox Money" during retirement.*

Now you've found the right town and the right neighborhood, how do you make sure you don't buy a money pit?

## Property Acquisition

You've probably heard the saying, *"You don't make money in real estate when you sell, you make money when you buy."*

What that means is that buying the right property for the right price is where you ensure a positive and profitable real estate investment.

The first part of buying right is getting the location right. The second part of buying right is knowing what you will invest in rehabbing a property and what will yield the best bang for the buck while reducing maintenance expenses over time.

If you haven't purchased hundreds of homes, then you might focus on the wrong things.

You might think that the kitchen, carpets, or paint make a difference. Your inspection might miss the biggest expense you'll face. Believe me, if you don't account for the right things, you'll end up with ongoing maintenance expenses that can zap your cash flow.

There are hundreds of different ways to go about rehabbing a property. Half of it is knowing what your goal is before you start.

If you are doing a rehab to flip a property to a home buyer for top dollar, you will focus on very different aspects of the home in order to get the highest price possible.

If you watch the Do-It-Yourself or Home Flipping TV shows, they are usually focused on rehabbing a home to get the best bang for the buck when they turn around and immediately sell the home.

If you're going to rehab a property for the purpose of renting it to a tenant, the parts of the home you fix and the quality of materials you will use, are very different from the home you would buy, fix, and immediately resell.

For example, with my approach of rehabbing for rental income, I would focus on identifying any possible plumbing issues and replacing pipes, drains and fixtures, including toilets.

The reason I do that is after years of experience, I know what will be most likely to cause tenant complaints and how to eliminate most of them before they can ever be a cause for concern. This becomes great for you because we are taking care of it before you even own the property.

Rehabbing a home can be very expensive. It's so very easy to "over rehab" a home and treat it like a home you are trying to flip immediately for a profit.

Almost as bad as over rehabbing a home is when you cut corners and under rehab.

You will spend more on the three or four service calls over a year to fix the toilet, than the drain, for example; and you'll wish you had done them both during the rehab phase. Service calls can, for the most part, be avoided when the rehab is done right. That is the key!

## How do you avoid the money pit?

From our experience, about 80% of all service calls that happen in a rental have something to do with water or water related damage.

Therefore, one of the main things you want to do when you rehab a property is fully inspect any part of the home that has to do with water or can lead to damage by water.

In many cases, we'll re-plumb the entire house or at least a good portion of it. From the water heater all the way down to the toilets, all the way up to the food disposal underneath the sink.

## Single Story or Two Story?

From a strict cost perspective, a two story home can appear to create more return for the initial investment, but experience tells a different story.

I know I've beat on this note again and again, but it's so critical that I can't let you miss it. The goal of this entire approach is consistent Mailbox Money. Because we're so clear on the objective, all decisions made in the Retire On Rent approach are measured against that standard.

What kind of house do we buy? The kind that will most reliably return long-term consistent cash flow.

So single story homes win out over multi level homes.

If you buy two story houses, they can add another set of variables simply because water runs to the second story.

The roof is another place where water damage often originates.

Part of buying a home is knowing if your roof is sound or if you would need to cover the cost of replacing the roof, which should be thoroughly inspected for before closing on the home.

What you're really looking for when rehabbing a home is to eliminate any potential future tenant issues having to do with water.

In addition to the service calls from water related issues, massive water damage, although often covered by insurance, can create a headache you don't want.

## Property Rehabilitation

Our process is very well put together so that the project manager doing the rehab knows exactly what issues the property manager is hoping to avoid.

Too often there is a substantial disconnect between what the property manager deals with and what issues are addressed at the rehab stage.

Before we ever acquire a home, we have the job inspected and estimated by our project manager. Because of our volume, we know that we can complete the rehab for about half the cost estimate that you would see from any other contractor.

Because we have spent well over a million dollars at the local home improvement store, we have really learned how to reduce the cost of our rehabs and where you can save money without cutting corners.

With a good system in place like ours we will often get better quality materials and instead of paying an outside contractor $20,000 to rehab the home, our team can do it for $10,000-$12,000.

What you spend on rehab matters. This alone can completely affect your rate of return because you have a significant amount more money invested in the property.

Beware that spending less and spending it on the wrong repairs and improvements will create as many problems as spending more and spending it on the wrong repairs and improvements.

Not only is it important to come in under budget, but it's also important that the money you do invest is invested in the right places.

These right places range from the fixtures, to the ceramic tiles, to the water supply lines, the GFI circuits and so on.

When you do the high volume that our team does and you have dialed in on what items you will almost always replace on the homes you buy you get the added benefit of bulk pricing on materials.

With that added benefit, with any home you buy, instead of worrying about going over budget, you get to decide what is the best thing for the long-term viability of a rental unit, knowing that because we bought in bulk, cost is not as much of a factor.

Some people will decide to do carpet, some people will decide to do ceramic, laminate or vinyl flooring; there isn't really a standard for those items when you're doing one or two or even a dozen homes.

However, if you're going to hold the property for the long term, you'd be wise to incorporate more durable surfaces inside the rental so that when you do have a turnover of tenants, you don't have to replace flooring each time, which can greatly reduce your annual rate of return.

One of the reasons so many people come to have my team do all this for them is they know that we have been down this road hundreds of times.

We invest our own money into this process every day and we've made all the mistakes with our own money. That is why working with a team that's doing this day in and day out and has been for years, is very different from trying to master this process on your own with 5-10 homes over several years.

It will take you 30+ houses and a decade to know what materials to buy, what materials you absolutely should not use, what items you should replace on every single house, how each item you replace is going to impact your investment 5- 10 years down the road.

Too often investors go cheap with everything, looking only at their costs one or two years from now. You can afford to make those kinds of mistakes in your first two quarters, and if you're not trying to make sure your Mother is taken care of for life.

I could not afford those kinds of mistakes.

On the other hand, many people spend way too much on the rehab. They forget that this home isn't going to be on a TV show. The main concern with my approach is to only worry about whether it's going to produce cash flow with minimal upkeep and maintenance.

---

*Think about property management*
*when you are rehabbing a home.*

---

Normally there is this separation between who will rehabilitate a home and who will screen the tenants and manage the property over time.

The problems that property managers run into is often a result of poor choices of materials and what to replace when the home was rehabilitated.

If you can have these two parts of your team work hand and hand, it gives a huge advantage to the person who wants to Retire On Rent and not become a general contractor and property manager.

## Why not go high end on properties?

I was connecting on a flight through Cincinnati, flying on Delta airlines.

I really wanted to get home that night because my son had an event the next day. That day I had only eaten a bag of chips for lunch and skipped dinner.

It was 10:30 at night and I'm about to eat my hand or my luggage, I was feeling that hungry.

While I am there in the Cincinnati airport there were only two choices for food that late at night. I didn't care too much about quality at that point, I just needed food.

The options were a sandwich place where I can get a mediocre sandwich for $10 or I could sit down and order some food and pay about $30 for a mediocre steak.

What was important was the fact that I was hungry and needed to eat.

Guess which option I and most other people chose? Yes, the $10 mediocre sandwich. That's where the masses will go as it fits in better with the situation (*at an airport late at night trying to get home and you just need food in your belly*).

In rental real estate this is very similar.

You don't need to have the highest quality house, it doesn't have to be the most beautiful house. You don't want something that is out of range for the average consumer.

Everyone needs housing and in the rental market, catering to the high end tenant doesn't provide the most consistent return on investment.

With the pretty homes, in the higher price range, you often have two or three months of vacancy every year and that absolutely destroys your rate of return.

If you would have a 12% rate of return for a full year, you are now down to 8% or even less if any vandalism happens to take place while that nice home sits vacant.

If you have a good quality home, that is very clean, that is rented for 36 months at a time and you only have a month of vacancy every three years, it will outperform a pretty home and have much lower upkeep costs between tenants.

## Property Management

What is the most important piece to the Retire On Rent system?

An incredible property management company is really the secret to making the Retire On Rent plan work.

Having a pretty property is not the answer.

Having the best materials in the home is not the answer.

Having the tenant set up on automatic draft is not the answer.

Hands down, the answer, the *"secret sauce"* if you will, is the quality of the property management company.

The number one thing that I would encourage you to find is a family owned and operated property management company.

These are the "ma and pa" shops that own properties themselves and they own the same type of properties that you would own.

They have their local team that keeps up on what is going on in the area that may affect your rental.

They know what's going on and they're not going to be steering you anywhere where there could be possible issues, because then they would have to deal with those issues. They usually have a vested interest in the performance of the property.

There's a saying in our property manager's office; *"Good tenants know good tenants."*

The police officers and the firefighters know other police officers and firefighters who may need a nice place to live.

They have good jobs and good tenants know other good tenants. One of the crucial keys of property management is the ability to cross rent properties to other tenants.

What that means is not only that the property management company needs to have a hand in how the property is rehabilitated, but they also need to make sure that they have a very proactive hand in the property location selection.

When the property management company has a vested interest in the property, because they own the same properties, they want the properties to rent and they want to get those great referrals from the great tenants.

The smart property manager wants their occupants to be rated very, very high. This results in less issues for them to deal with, less damage to properties and more opportunity to cross rent any vacant units to the tenant's friends.

The nicer looking homes will generate over 50 phone calls from some of their advertising. The goal is not to find one tenant for that one home that they're advertising.

The goal is to take those incoming calls and find out what would be best for that caller and then direct them to other homes that are near by that would be a better fit.

This isn't a bait and switch, there are other homes that are similar to the home they advertised, but it may not have as many upgrades and be a better fit  for that persons' budget.

With my team, we found scalability on the property management side right after we began to manage about 80 to 100 homes.

That's where the scalability became clear and where we bounced on economies of scale and the property management became a lot easier. That took a long time and a lot of mistakes, but now it runs like a well oiled machine.

## Accounting and Auditing

How do you want the property management company to handle the money when you're looking for property management?

Property management companies will have a variety of different ways to take in money. They may allow the tent to do online payments or automatic recurring online payments. Some tenants may want to pay rent on a weekly basis.

Other property managers intelligently locate their property management office in the city.

They're going to have tenants that will be driving in to drop their rent off at the local property management office and the tenant is going to want to be able to pick up a receipt when they drop off payment.

A very good property management company will be able to direct deposit rental income into a property owner's accounts.

That's essential, even if it does take away the experience of actually going and getting your "Mailbox Money" out of your mailbox.

## Special Considerations for Self Managed IRA Investors

If you want to Retire On Rent with a self directed IRA, you cannot be the property manager of your own properties. You must use a third party, so choose wisely.

## Keeping the Books Clean

Property management fees can range from anywhere from 7%-10%, that's the average property management fee for a single-family home.

With a higher revenue producing rental, the percentage of rent charged as a fee is typically lower. For example, a $3K a month rental in CA might only be at 7%, whereas the $800 month rental in the Midwest may be closer to 10%.

Keep in mind that a property management company isn't a highly profitable business.

Many property management companies don't break even until they get over 100 homes. For a great company that screens tenants correctly and takes care of the property well, you are going to pay about a 9% or 10% property management fee and it's well worth it.

The next thing you want to ensure is handled correctly by your property manager is repairs.

Most property management companies will be very proactive on a property and respond to maintenance calls promptly.

They'll have a limit to what they can spend to keep a property up in good repair in order to collect a solid rent for a property owner.

As I mentioned before, a wax ring on a toilet is very inexpensive and a property management company would not expect to call you for permission to fix a leak in the toilet that a simple wax ring would remedy.

That's something that they would respond to immediately.

A good property management company would then deduct it from your rent, and deposit in your account the balance with an accounting breakdown of the expense.

If purchased in the right way, even with a mortgage, the property should maintain itself on a monthly basis.

The gross income comes in and the property management company will take out any property management fee.

Therefore, a good property management company would not make any income on a vacant property.

They only win when you are winning. Be careful of any other type of contract. You don't want to pay 10% up front, just to find out that they cut corners on the tenant and now you have to spend money to evict a non-paying tenant and then rehab the property that the bad tenant damaged, all while the property manager you hired was paid up front for this mess.

Remember, their job is to get it rented to a great tenant who will pay on time and treat the house well. They should only benefit from the property when you do.

Next, the property manager will deduct any expenses related to property maintenance. The rest would be for your net Mailbox Money.

The property owner is responsible for their own property taxes and insurance. If you use a mortgage to buy a rental, then you can have your mortgage company pay those for you as well.

The property manager would then report to you an accounting of any work orders.

Any wise property manager has a thorough move-in and a move-out process, for legal reasons.

You don't need a bunch of *"he said, she said"* going on when a tenant is moving out and claims the house was trashed when they moved in.

A thorough move in process will reduce that possibility. This ensures that tenants know that the property was clean when they moved in and expected to be clean when they move out.

Just as you do when you use a rental car, you will walk around the car, make note of any damage so that when it's returned, any existing damage is not blamed on you and likewise, any new damage can be credited to you.

---

## The right team for the system

---

One of the keys to know that you are working with the right team is if they have a vested interest. Specifically, do they invest or do they have ownership in the same properties you do?

If so, out of necessity they're going to develop systems that work very well to limit costs and improve the quality of the tenants.

For example, I developed systems for helping my Mother's investment because I was very emotionally tied to the result. I was willing to invest in the same type of homes that I was assisting her to invest in.

Really, what you're looking for is the property management to be local, family owned and operated and that owns the same type of properties that you do.

If you're keeping count, and you've read from the beginning of this book to here, then you'll note this is the third time I've said the same thing. I don't suffer from short term memory loss. I'm trying to impress upon you a VERY IMPORTANT POINT.

It is a painful lesson I learned the hard way. You want the local, family business to manage your properties. They're not going anywhere and you know that things will only get better over time.

## The power of scale

Scalability is the main reason why it's important that the property manager is local and knows the market. This is what I looked for-both for my success and for my Mom's success.

When the property manager knows the market and has solid systems, then scaling to manage 100 more homes is easier and also reduces the cost for all the owners whose homes they manage.

As an illustration of the economies of scale, one of my friends owns a franchise here locally in my town.

After the first year of running that franchise, he bought a second franchise location with the same franchisor.

That allowed him to buy supplies at a greater discount as he was now purchasing double and it allowed him to have one general manager cover both locations.

From employees, to supplies, to whatever you need to run the franchise, when you are able to scale like that, systems tend to improve and costs tend to go down.

Rarely will you see someone that owns just one Subway franchise in Charlotte, North Carolina, then another single Subway franchise in Dallas, Texas and their third in Seattle, Washington.

The local scalability is essential for a property management company to handle routine maintenance calls, screening, collections, etc.

If you were my Mother or my best friend, I would refer you to a locally owned and operated property management company. They have the boots on the ground, they know how to get things done quickly and inexpensively.

They also know, for example, how to get materials at a wholesale cost if possible, and they know, even down to the store managers at the local home improvement shops.

## That's Confidential Information...

The best way to find out if you will be hiring the right property management company is to first find out if they are local or if they work from the next county over. Then, ask them for references so you can speak with their customers, whose properties they are managing.

A successful local company with a long history is going to be able to give you plenty of referrals. One that hesitates or says, *"that's confidential information"* is usually covering their lack of experience or poor reputation.

Basically, in a great property management company, what you will notice is a theme of transparency.

You will be able to notice if they have this theme of transparency from the beginning. When you are interviewing a property management company, it will be apparent that they are either transparent or guarded.

As you talk to their references you will be able to ask direct questions about transparency, reporting and how issues are handled.

Be sure to ask the references questions about the things that the property manager does for them from the screening to the day to day management.

Find out about the terms of their agreement with the property manager and what they do and don't like about them.

How you determine if it's a good property management company is through conversation with third parties who have decided to work with the property manager.

## An online system

To make it easy on yourself, find a property manager that has an online system that by using your own login and password, you can find out what's going on with your properties.

If you have a question at midnight on a weekend, you can go online and see exactly what's going on with your property.

Additionally, once a month you should get a profit and loss statement.

Now you have a good idea of the component parts of the Retire On Rent system and the team members that support it.

You understand why our clients don't worry about tenants and toilets like most folks who are trying to create Mailbox Money with rentals.

You understand the common myths and pitfalls that give rental income a bad name.

Most of all, you now know why the Retire On Rent system isn't like any other approach you've seen before. You know why I'm able to say I kept my promise to my Dad.

# Chapter 9

# TWO WAYS TO BUY

I usually see two approaches when people decide to take advantage of our Retire On Rent system.

The first approach is to qualify for and obtain mortgage financing to purchase the property. The second approach is to pay cash.

## Buying with Financing

Each approach will be slightly different depending on what quarter of life you are in. If you are in your first or second quarter of life (25-45 years old) you very well could put as little down as possible, buy several homes with mortgages and by the time you are ready to retire, you could have several homes paid off just by the rental income alone.

Most Americans hit their prime "income earning years" between 40-60 years old. When you get to your late 30's and early 40's, you're in a stage of life where you may be able to easily obtain mortgage financing on several homes.

For those in the third and fourth quarter of "pre-retirement" you too can take advantage of using mortgage financing to increase the leverage of your current assets, but you will be taking on additional risk that may cost you too much, too late in life to be able to fully overcome.

The last decade has taught us that until you have the property paid off, there is always risk of losing a property to foreclosure.

The return on your down payment invested when using a mortgage is pretty good with the markets that I specialize in.

You can borrow money for a much lower percentage than the annual rate of return. Let's say your interest rate is about 6% on a non-owner occupied loan.

Keep in mind, these are non-owner occupied loans, these are not owner occupied loans. What that means is that your rates will be a little bit higher and your down payments will usually be about 20%-30% of the purchase price. Let me go over a simple scenario of how this might look.

I'll use very rough numbers here in order to keep the illustration simple, yet accurate and assume you are required to put 20% down in order to get your financing.

In this example, let's assume you are investing in a home that has gone through our Retire On Rent system. The purchase price is $100,000 and you put down $20,000 to close escrow. The average monthly rental income is $1,000 a month if we are using a 12% annual gross return.

Your interest costs on a $80,000 loan at5.5% are about $450 a month. Let's assume another $350 a month for a maintenance reserve, insurance, management costs, etc.

Here is how the first year Return on Investment looks:

+ $12,000 ($1,000 x 12) first year rental income
- $5,400 ($450 x 12) interest expense
- $4,200 ($350 x 12) misc expenses
 $3,500 in cash flow and principal reduction

---

*$3,500 / $20,000 invested = 17.5% annual ROI*

---

When you look at the numbers and factor in the amazing tax benefits of depreciation, effectively that ROI going up, you aren't going to find many other collateralized investments that can generate a annual ROI of over 17.5%, which will increasse over time as more principle each year gets applied to the mortgage balance. (By the way, we didn't factor in ANY appriciation or rental increases...)

So what is the limitation if you have 20% for a down payment on 20 homes?

Currently, no traditional mortgage lender will allow a borrower to have more than ten mortgaged properties showing up under their social security number. That being said, we do have access to some more creative financing for those of you that are interested. Contact my office directly for access to these programs.

In the years past, an LLC could carry a mortgage. These days, it's very, very difficult to get a loan using anything but your own social security number.

The underwriter that looks at a specific loan scenario needs to look at a specific social security number and their income, and their debt to income ratio, even when you are seeking non-owner occupied financing and putting down 20%-30% of the purchase price.

What some people will do right about that age where they decide they are done having kids is say, "Instead of upgrading to a bigger house and raising our monthly payments and our car has over 80,000 miles, but instead of getting a new car we're going to drive it for two more years".

What they might do is get their bonus, and instead of upgrading their house or get a new car, they might use some of that money to go ahead and buy a rental house.

That's a long term focus and it isn't a strategy where you hope to cash out next year or the year after. You are planning for long term wealth and cash flow.

Some of the folks I have worked with have said to me, "*I want to buy a house when the kids are younger and get a fifteen year mortgage so instead of putting money into a college savings account, I am putting it into an asset that is helping me accelerate the growth of my child's college fund while producing cash flow for year to come.*"

If that approach resonates with you, here is how it works.

With a traditional mortgage, a 30 year or even a 15 year mortgage, you're going to receive monthly cash flow from the property.

You're goal is to reduce your interest expenses as much as possible (*assuming you aren't in need of any cash flow from the property*) so instead of pocketing the net cash flow, you're putting every dime back into paying off the mortgage faster.

Essentially, your tenant is assisting you with funding a good portion of your child's college fund.

With this type of scenario, time is your friend.

The younger you start, the better.

If your child is under ten years old and you are able to buy a property with a 15 or 30 year mortgage and you have a great property manager, which means you have great tenants, your mortgage will be paid down substantially by the time your child goes to college.

In addition, you're going to be getting depreciation on your taxes and there is the possibility of appreciation, even though we aren't banking on it.

When using the mortgage approach, you're basically borrowing money at ~6% to buy a cash producing asset (using the numbers in my area) that can generate a 12%-15% annual return on the entire cash out of pocket.

Try borrowing money at 6% to buy stocks. Then, try to find stocks that produce a 12%-15% return, year after year.

Call your loan officer at your bank and say *"I'm really interested in Microsoft stock, I want to buy $100,000 worth of stock. Can you get me a $70,000 loan at 6% interest to go by Microsoft if I put in $30,000?"*, and they'll laugh and probably hang up on you.

---

## Buying with Cash

---

The second approach, buying with cash, is the ideal way to invest if you plan to Retire On Rent without the risk associated with having a mortgage.

It is an obvious limitation for many people. Some of the folks I've worked with have millions to invest, while others have less than $100K.

In either case, they can both benefit, but would use different strategies to get to where they want.

Most of the folks I work with, who are in their fourth quarter of life, prefer to pay cash for any properties they invest in.

---

## Using your IRA to invest

---

The common approach when purchasing a property in a self-directed IRA is a cash purchase.

What I mean by that is there's very little leverage available when investing in an IRA.

Unless you can get a private mortgage without any personal guarantee, you won't find mortgages available for the IRA.

That means that if you have a $100,000 balance in your IRA and the purchase price of the home you are buying is $100,000, you're going to be able to use the $100,000 in the IRA to make the purchase of one home.

There are private investors out there that will lend to a self directed IRA. As long as you have 40% to put down, they'll finance 60% of the purchase price, even without a personal guarantee by you (remember, you can't personally guarantee a loan when the asset is being acquired in the IRA).

Here is why these private lenders are often willing to make a loan to an IRA without having any personal guarantee.

If that lender has to foreclose on the IRA for non-payment, they are pretty confident that through the foreclosure process, they will get back 60% of that properties' value, which is equivalent to their entire loan balance.

*"I don't have a lot of money in my IRA, how do I start using a self directed IRA if I don't have enough to buy a home right now?"*

Theoretically, if you don't have enough money in an IRA to buy a home outright, but you have enough to cover a 40-50% down payment and then have the rest financed, your IRA can own the property.

Another approach would be to do a joint venture with multiple IRAs (assuming you have one and your spouse has one) where your IRA puts in part of the down payment and your spouse's IRA puts in the balance and your IRAs both have ownership and benefit from the property.

One approach that is useful if you have younger children is to do a joint purchase using your child's Educational Savings Account.

You could create a Coverdell Education Savings Account (ESA) for each of your children, which allow you to fund $5,000 a year. After a couple years or if you have multiple children, you can begin to acquire homes together using both your self directed IRA and your child's Coverdell ESA.

Let's assume you have two children and you set them both up with Coverdell ESAs and fund the maximum of $5,000 each for both funds in August.

In January, just a few months from setting up the funds, you can add an additional $5,000 in each ESA and reach your max contribution for that year.

In a matter of just a few months, you have $20,000 between the two ESAs, plus let's assume you have $20K in a self directed IRA.

If you find a private investor to fund 60% of the purchase price, without requiring a personal guarantee, you can use $10,000 from one child's ESA, $10,000 from the other's and $20,000 from your self directed IRA to acquire a $100,000 home.

This breaks the ownership up into three parts.

One child's ESA owns 25%, the other ESA owns 25% and your IRA owns 50% of the net income and net gain if/ when the property is sold.

## Why don't people invest in real estate?

In the movie 'Snow White and the Seven Dwarfs', at one time the dwarfs said something to the effect of "we don't like what we don't know, in fact we hate it".

Really what they're saying is, ignorance isn't really bliss.

One of the reasons some people don't enjoy rental real estate is they don't have the knowledge, the systems, the staff, or the team. Therefore they're nervous. Therefore it's an unknown and they feel it's "safer" to not get involved.

There is a safe way to get involved in investing.

The system and team I have put in place is kind of like your GPS navigation.

Not the old style GPS, I am talking about Google's newest and best turn by turn, down to the correct lane to be in GPS navigation.

Imagine you are in a town which you've never been to before and the GPS navigation in your rental car is guiding you to your luxurious hotel where you will be staying.

It's going to show you the fastest route to get there, avoiding traffic and congested roads, while using the least amount of fuel.

It tells you where to go, turn by turn and even which lane to be in to avoid any last minute changes that could cause an accident, delay, and cost you money.

It will even tell you which side of the road your final destination will be on.

Because we've already navigated rental real estate investing and done this hundreds and hundreds of times, we can guide you the same way.

I'd like to share with you a copy of our Map that we use to navigate folks through this process without pain and without the fear and uncertainty that usually comes with doing something of this magnitude on your own for the first time.

Text **MAP** to **(317) 900-4228** and I'll send you a copy of our map.

If you have a map and you follow it, you're going to end up avoiding 95% of the mistakes that your predecessors have made as well as increase the overall rate of return from not making those costly mistakes.

---

*The "turn key" solution to
the Retire On Rent strategy.*

---

Some people say they really want six pack abs.

Hang with me, abs have a lot to do with the Retire On Rent system.

These people will go to the gym, work out, run miles and miles a day and eat chicken and broccoli. However, if they could just take a pill that had no side effects and the next day have six pack abs, nice shoulders and arms and good looking legs, most people would choose to just pop the pill.

Unfortunately, they have not yet created a no side- effects six pack abs pill.

However, with my team that executes the Retire On Rent system, we have essentially created the equivalent of a "pill" that generates the results you want.

Will you still have to manage your property manager and keep in touch? Sure. Are there any guarantees? Grow up, of course not. Will you be spending your weekends at your rental? You better not be!

You want the cash flow, you want the depreciation to offset income taxes, you want the upside potential... but you don't want to deal with all the moving parts.

You want someone else to do the heavy lifting for you and then simply direct deposit the rent for you each month.

As a turn-key rental provider, we do everything for you, from acquisition and rehab, to tenant screening and property management. Money shows up in your account every month without having to lift a finger.

What we've done is taken this idea of a rental home and through a certain amount of trial and error, which has created tons of real world experience, we have developed processes, systems and strategies that minimize risk and maximize gain for the investors we work with.

To be transparent, we benefit by making a small margin from rehabbing the home (*however, even with our profit margin, our buying power and discounts make it so you still are better off than spending your own time and money to rehab a home*) and also grow our property management portfolio.

We are still actively acquiring properties as well, so you know we are in the same business, side by side with you as investors.

We are always looking for ways to reduce costs and improve processes.

# Chapter 10

# WHY ACT NOW?

Baby boomers are a large population, with 76 million people born between 1946 and 1964.

For the most part pensions are a thing of the past, so many of these baby boomers are going to rely on the government to not only provide them a monthly income, but also take care of their health care.

It's going to overburden the system.

Tack on top that according to minimum distribution of this generation, they are going to be removing their money from the stock market as they turn 70 and a half.

This uncertainty in the market has caused a lot of people to want to diversify their income sources in retirement. They want to make sure that if the stock market is rocked in some way, or if the overall value of their portfolio decreases, they want to insure themselves by buying hard assets.

So why not just buy gold or silver or precious gems if hard assets have less overall risk? One of the reasons why most people planning for retirement don't put too much money into gold, silver or precious gems is **they don't produce a monthly income**.

While you may find those hard assets have years where the return on investment is good, they do not kick up a monthly income and they aren't as predictable as, for example, rental income.

Every single month, I make rental income on my property and over the long term, my rental property will appreciate.

In fact, in spite of the recent rock up and down in the real estate market, the average over the past 40 years has been 3.7% annual appreciation.

Real estate acts as a hedge against inflation, but it also is an income producer, which makes it unique compared to most investments you will find.

The good news is, with the Retire On Rent system and the team that surrounds it, owning rental real estate is not as risky, it's not labor intensive and it becomes a truly passive investment.

The system and team I have in place is no different than how your other investments are managed. Someone, somewhere has to manage them or you could lose money.

Whether that be a financial planner, stock broker or someone else, they will manage your investments for you so you can focus on retirement or other things that you enjoy doing or are good at doing.

## *How can this go bad?*

With a traditional purchase of a home where the buyer is getting mortgage financing, the property has to be appraised. That means a third party has to inspect the property and come to the conclusion that the home is worth the purchase price.

One way that you're going to be protecting yourself as a cash buyer is to always get an appraisal to ensure it is worth the price you are paying. The neutral third party validating the purchase price is important to ensure you aren't over paying.

You remember from eighth grade that supply and demand determine price.

But sometimes supply can be manipulated to mess with the price. That's why they sell water bottles at the baseball field for $4, because they have manipulated supply and know what the demand is. This manipulation is what drives prices outside what folks would normally accept.

This is very hard to do with real estate.

Real estate is valued against the neighborhood and there is no event like a baseball game. You have a third party evaluating your property, which gives the investor comfort in knowing that it is an unbiased judgment of the property value.

The next thing that you should always do, no matter how new the home is or when it was last remodeled, is to order a full property inspection.

In order to limit your risk in a rental property, you're looking at not only a home that has been third party appraised, but that is also third party inspected.

Beware of anyone that discourages you from getting a home inspection, especially if that comes from anyone related to the seller's side of the transaction.

A home inspection is done by a third party who will go through the home, typically for a couple of hours, inspecting the roof to the foundation and everything in between.

The home inspection is optional. However, it is crucial to know what repairs, if any, need to be done before you agree on your final purchase.

When you buy a property that is already rented to a tenant you should also complete your due diligence on the current tenant, their payment history, their original rental application and the terms of the lease.

---

*What could happen if values don't stay up, if something traumatic happens to the economy?*

---

The best way to hedge against a rocky economy is to have good enough margins and to ensure that you are investing in an area with smaller overall swings in market value.

For Mom, I look to buy a property that generates 10%-15% of the gross rent in annual rental income. I also look for "good property" that I know won't require expensive upkeep.

What happens if my property declines by 20% over the next two years?

Is it possible? Of course, we've seen that happen in the last decade and in some places values dropped almost in half of what they were at their peak.

In rental real estate, you'll notice that your rental income will in a sense "hedge" against the drop in the home value.

Basically, if the market does drop, you can "rent your way out" of the declining market.

Here is why...

My mortgage payment is fixed for 15 or 30 years and isn't going to go up just because the property value goes down.

If I'm cash flow positive from day one, does that mortgage value change because the value of my property goes down? No. What about the rent rates? Will those go up or down during this time?

This is may sound counterintuitive, but what we've experienced with a rental is that when the home prices go down, the rental income will actually go up.

In a declining market there are more people who would have considered buying in the past that decide to sit on the sidelines until values stop going down. This means that over all, there are more renters looking for homes.

Many of these potential renters are replacing their $2,000 a month mortgage for a $1,000-$1,500 a month renal. It goes back to simple economics of supply and demand.

The competition for being approved for a lease goes up in a declining home value market. Therefore, rents would go up, even if home prices may have declined.

I was recently talking to a loan officer and a direct lender who does collectively about a billion dollars in business a year.

He was saying the big trend going forward is more people are less interested in buying homes and more interested in renting homes because of what they just saw with the last big swings in the real estate market.

They're kind of in shock over what happened with real estate prices.

So the idea of buying a home has become less attractive to them.

This is good news for you. There are going to continue to be more renters and you have to decide if you want to be the one receiving the rents.

A good property management company will have the ability to slowly and intelligently increase rent.

There are some tenants that have better vehicles, bigger screen TV, and shiner Harley Davidson's in their garage, and they are what I would call Owner/Tenants. They are tenants, but they treat the home as their own. Many of them previously owned a home and got accustomed to fixing little things around the house and they are happy paying $1,000 a month in rent instead of paying $1,500+ to own.

They mow the lawn and they take care of the home inside and out for the most part. There are a variety of different circumstances that can produce that owner/tenant.

That's another reason why the single-family marketplace is, in my opinion, better than the apartment marketplace.

You don't usually have former single family home owners downgrade to an apartment, however, a good number of the tenants in the market for a single family home have previously owned their own home.

This also gives you a greater ability to raise rents and not lose good tenants.

Most of them have their nice cars or trucks and have a little extra disposable incomes where raising rents 5% one year isn't going to break the bank for them.

As long as you picked the right location, where there are good schools and amenities close by, you're going to be able to keep up the rents at market rate without fear of having turnover of tenants.

It's amazing what the right location will do for attracting good tenants. We have had to sign five year leases with some tenants because they wanted to make sure their kids didn't have to switch schools. Of course, we also love to sign five year leases and build in a 3% minimal annual rent increase.

If you don't have a clear goal, sit down and decide what you want to achieve and in what time frame. Having specific goals will bring you clarity on what you want as well as what needs to happen to get you to where you want to go.

Be extremely clear. What do you really want in the next 5 years? What do you really want out of your retirement? What do you want your retirement to look like? Will you be traveling, living close to family and enjoying the grandkids?

Then analyze your current path. If what you're doing right now works for you, and you're slowly developing a monthly income right now off your current action plan and you feel it is hedged against many of the risks we've talked about, then you might not need rental real estate.

If you're 40 or 50 years old and you don't have a plan or your current plan is solely based on the stock market, you need to have a strategy session with someone like me.

You need to have a conversation with someone who knows the questions to ask and the plan to create, based off of your specific goals and time frame.

Be willing to open up and realize you may not understand everything that's involved with planning how much money you'll actually need to retire. Be aware that real estate is a time tested and proven path to true retirement.

The way you get to the point of having a portfolio of homes that fund your retirement is with that first single house. One bite at a time.

When you get going and realize how much going down this path will benefit you, you'll probably echo the sentiment of many of the folks we help and say, "I wish I would have started this 10 years ago".

Start the conversation with your spouse or with whomever is a part of your retirement plan. No matter where you are, start developing a monthly income, even if it's with one single home.

Soon you'll be saying what our other investors say, "Do I want to buy another car or do I want to buy another home for $65,000?" That $65,000 house can then very easily produce enough monthly rental income to purchase a $65,000 SUV in a short amount of time, if that is what you choose.

When it's all said and done, you will own the house free and clear, and that house will buy that SUV for you, so that you will also own it free and clear.

## Who should get started?

First of all, you have to have enough cash to buy a home, or you have to be able to qualify for a conventional or private loan.

So, if you're currently broke and you don't have a job, savings or retirement, then you may need to put other plans in place first in order to get to a place where you can begin to invest in properties that will allow you to Retire On Rent.

I talk to many owners who always assumed that they weren't qualified to start their investment portfolio in their 50s, but they could have easily started in their 20s or 30s and they would have already had their first couple of homes paid off.

The process of getting a rental loan takes very little time and isn't as complex as many assume.

The three biggest things the lender will look at are Debt to Income ratio, down payment and credit.

Obviously, the asset has to be worth the purchase price which will be verified via an appraisal.

---

## Next Steps

---

Regardless of where you find yourself today, the key is to get started.

As they say, "*A thousand mile journey begins with the first step.*"

I'd like to help you with that first step.

Begin today by texting **PLAN** to **(317) 900-4228** and a member of my team will work with you one on one to create a game plan specifcaly tailored to you.

Wishing you the best and that all your promises may be kept.

-M.D.